RUDE JOKES AROUND THE OFFICE

rhys eption

strathearn

LONDON • NEW YORK • TORONTO • SYDNEY

Strathearn Publishing

PO Box 44, Slough, Berkshire, SL1 4YN

Trade Distribution by W. Foulsham & Co. Ltd

The Publishing House, Bennetts Close, Cippenham, Slough, Berkshire, SL1 5AP, England

ISBN 0-572-03029-0

Copyright © 2004 Strathearn Publishing Ltd

All rights reserved.

The Copyright Act prohibits (subject to certain very limited exceptions) the making of copies of any copyright work or of a substantial part of such a work, including the making of copies by photocopying or similar process. Written permission to make a copy or copies must therefore normally be obtained from the publisher in advance. It is advisable also to consult the publisher if in any doubt as to the legality of any copying which is to be undertaken.

Printed in Great Britain by Cox & Wyman Ltd, Reading, Berkshire

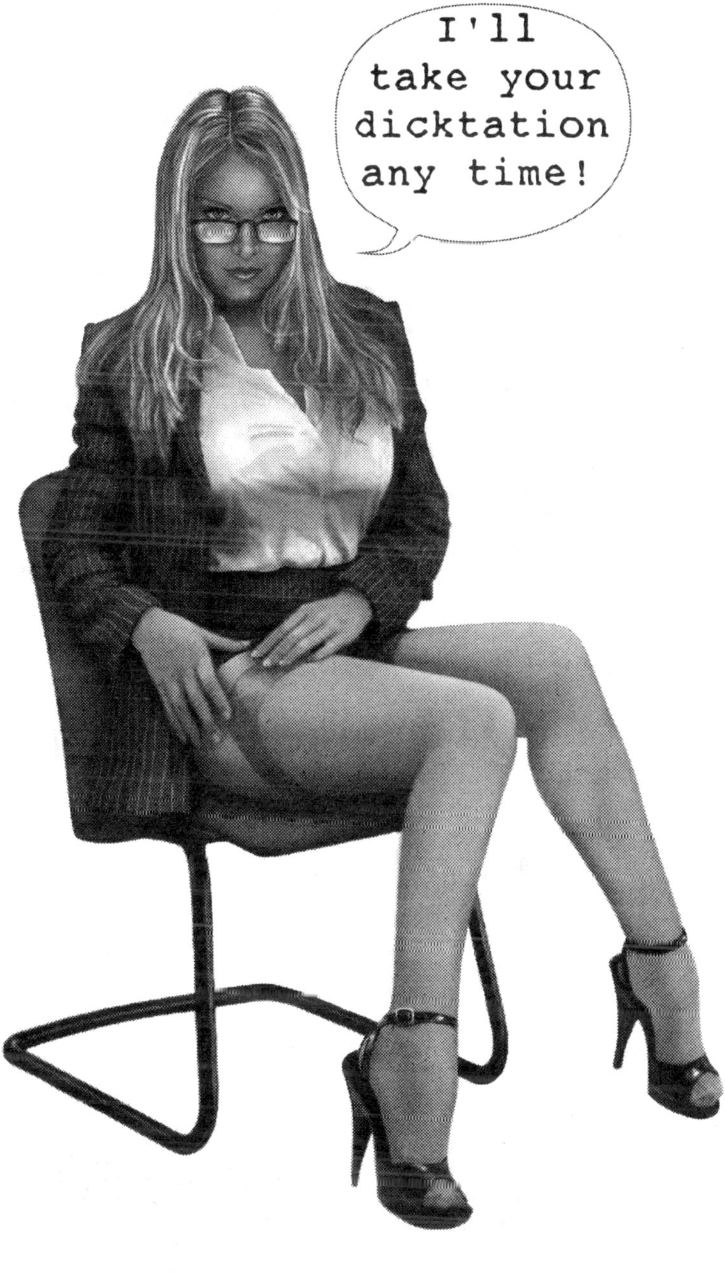
I'll take your dicktation any time!

A secretary is in hospital with appendicitis and is visited by one of her fellow office workers.

'How are things at the office, Claudia?' asks the secretary.

'It's fine. The others are sharing your work. Jodie is making the coffee, Sharon is reading all your magazines and Tricia is fucking the boss.'

Stuart rings his office and speaks to his boss.

'I can't come to work today, I am really sick. I've got a headache and my stomach is playing up as well.'

'Oh, damn,' replies his boss. 'I really need you at work today. When I'm sick I find that having sex with my wife always makes me feel better. Why don't you try that?'

A couple of hours later Stuart rings the office again.

'I did just what you said and I feel great. I'll be at work in 15 minutes. By the way – I love your new stair carpet.'

What's the difference between oral sex at the office and anal sex?

Oral sex makes your day, anal sex makes your hole weak.

How is a randy secretary like a condom?

Both spend more time in your wallet than on your dick.

Mr Jackson, the president of a large corporation, called his vice-president into his office.

'We're making some cutbacks, Dave,' he explained, 'so either Jack or Suzanne will have to be laid off. You have to choose between them.'

'That's a tough one,' Dave replied. 'Suzanne is my best worker, but Jack has a wife and three kids. Let me think about it overnight.'

So the next morning Dave waited for his employees to arrive. Suzanne was the first to come in, so Dave said,

'Suzanne, I've got a problem. You see, I've got to lay you or Jack off and I don't know what to do.'

'You'd better jack off,' replied Suzanne. 'I've got a headache.'

Why is the office 'bike' like take-away fried chicken?

By the time you've finished with the breast and thighs, all you have left is a greasy box to put your bone in.

What's the difference between the boss's wife, his mistress and a prostitute?

Spitting, swallowing and gargling.

A man gets laid off from his job, so he tells his wife that in order to pay the bills, she has to work the streets. Seeing no other option, she reluctantly agrees. He tells her he'll be in the car across the street to keep an eye on her. The first night, a car pulls up and the driver asks her,

'How much for a lay?'

'Umm, just gimmee a sec,' she says and runs across the street to ask her husband.

'Just charge him £100,' he says, so she runs back and tells the punter.

'Too much,' says the punter. 'How much for a blow job?'

Once again, she runs across to ask her husband. 'Charge him £80, ' he says.

Still the punter says, 'Too much. How much for a hand job?'

Her husband says, 'Oh, what the hell, charge him £60.'

The guy in the car agrees, but when he pulls out his massive penis, the wife says, 'Hold on a sec,' and runs back to her husband.

'Are you sure we can't lend him £40?'

WHAT DO YOU CALL A RANDY SECRETARY WITH A RUNNY NOSE?

Full.

What should you do if the typist at the office party starts smoking?

Slow down and use a lubricant.

Two guys were discussing the girls in the photocopy room.

'Mary's just a slag,' insisted Jim, 'but Sally's a real bitch.'

'What makes you say that?' asked Sam.

'Mary will sleep with anyone, but Sally will sleep with anyone but me!'

Glenn had worked in a pickle factory for some years. One day he confessed to his wife that he had a terrible compulsion to stick his penis into the pickle slicer. Horrified, she tried to make him see a sex therapist but he said he would be too embarrassed so he'd try to sort it out on his own.

A couple of weeks later, he came home looking absolutely ashen.

'What on earth is wrong, Glenn?' asked his wife.

'You remember I told you about my compulsion,' he replied.

'Oh my God, Glenn, you didn't?' she gasped. 'What happened?'

'I got the sack!'

'No! What happened with the pickle slicer?'

'She got the sack too.'

HOW DOES THE BOSS MAKE HIS WIFE CRY WHILE HE'S MAKING LOVE?

HE RINGS HER UP AND TELLS HER.

What's six inches long, two inches wide, and drives women wild?

A cash bonus.

The chairman of a big multi-national is on a business trip and he phones home to talk to his wife. The maid answers the phone.

'Can I speak to my wife please?' he says.

'No. I'm afraid she's in bed with her lover at the moment.'

'What!' he screams. 'Listen to me and you can earn five thousand quid. Take my shotgun, go upstairs and shoot them both.'

He hears two muffled shots, then the maid comes back to the phone.

'Where can I put the bodies?' she asks.

'Bury them in the back garden by the pool.'

'What pool?'

'That is 24 Acacia Terrace ... ?'

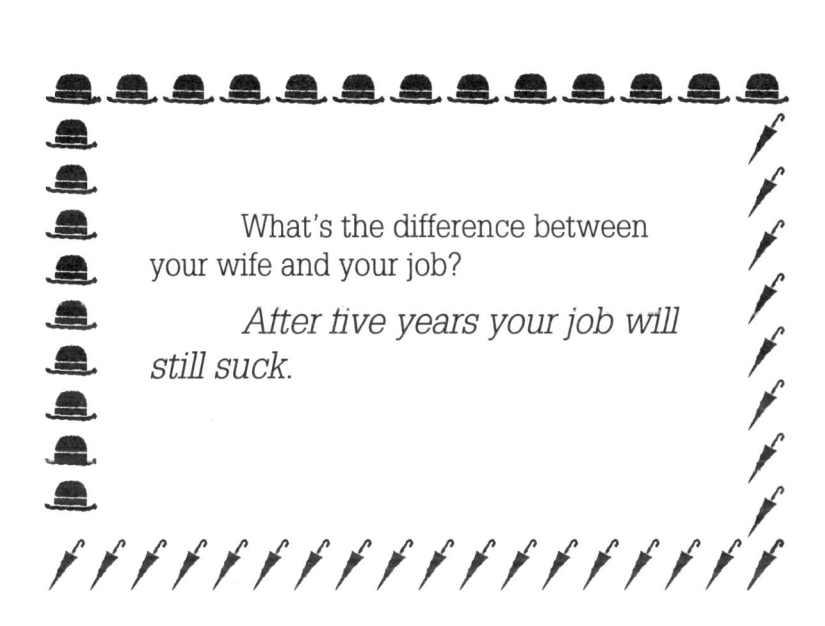

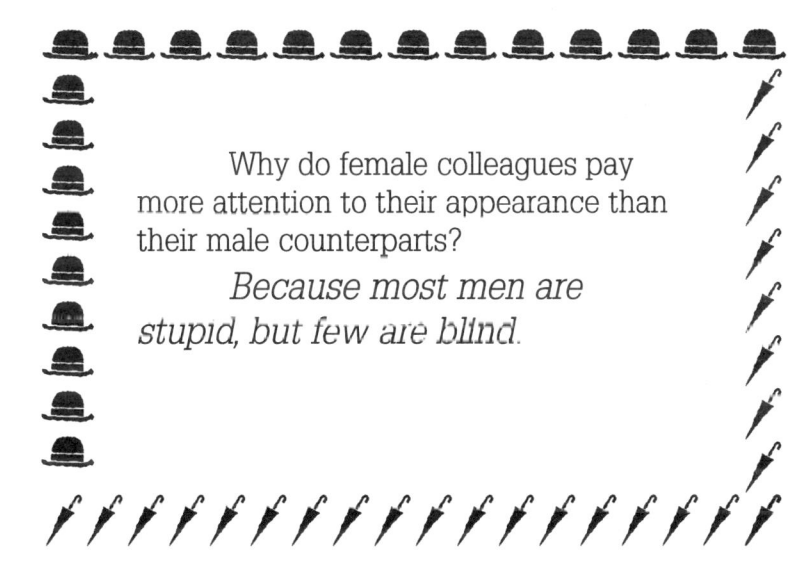

What's the difference between your wife and your job?

After five years your job will still suck.

Why do female colleagues pay more attention to their appearance than their male counterparts?

Because most men are stupid, but few are blind.

How do you annoy your girlfriend during sex?

Phone her.

How are fat girls and mopeds alike?

They're both fun to ride until your colleagues find out.

WHAT DO YOU SAY TO THE BOSS WHEN HE HAS LEFT HIS FLIES UNDONE?

You've got Windows on your laptop.

HOW CAN YOU TELL IF YOUR SECRETARY IS DEAD?

THE SEX IS THE SAME BUT THE FILING PILES UP.

REASONS WHY THE PENIS DEMANDED A SALARY INCREASE

I do physical labour.

I work at great depths.

I plunge head first into everything I do.

I do not get weekends off or public holidays.

I work in a damp environment.

I don't get paid overtime.

I work in a dark place with poor ventilation.

I work in high temperatures.

My work exposes me to contagious diseases.

REASONS WHY THE PENIS DIDN'T GET A SALARY INCREASE

You do not work eight hours at a time.

You fall asleep on the job.

You don't always follow management instructions.

You don't stay in your allocated position and often visit other areas.

You don't take the initiative – you need to be stimulated in order to start working.

You leave the workplace in a mess at the end of your shift.

You don't always observe the safety regulations, such as wearing the correct protective clothing.

You'll retire well before reaching 65.

You're unable to work double shifts.

You sometimes leave your position before you have completed the day's work.

You have been seen entering and leaving the workplace carrying two suspicious-looking bags.

♂

What's a drawing pin?

A smartie with a hard on.

How is sex with a colleague like a calculator?

Subtract clothes.
Add desk.
Divide legs and multiply.

Things you should never say to your boss when he's naked

'You know they have surgery to fix that.'

'Wow, and your feet are so big.'

'It's OK, we'll work around it.'

'Will it squeak if I squeeze it?"

'Can I be honest with you?'

'This explains your car.'

'At least this won't take long.'

'I never saw one like that before.'

'But it still works, right?'

'Why don't we skip right to the cigarettes?'

'It's a good thing you have so many other talents.'

Why does it suck to be the boss's penis?

The boss strangles you all the time.

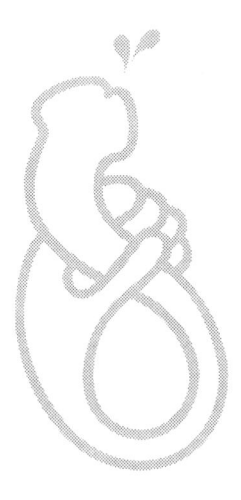

Why do British Rail employees never need to use a condom?

Because they always pull out on time.

The Boss's Evening Expenses on an Overseas Trip

Cover charge:	£15.00
Round of drinks:	£23.00
Table dance:	£30.00
Another round of drinks:	£23.00
Couch dance and tips:	£50.00
A round of shots:	£34.00
Another round of drinks:	£23.00
Lap dance and hand job:	£100.00
Private dance and hotel room:	£500.00
Sending her on her way without having to cuddle or listen to her:	Priceless!

A lawyer married a woman who had previously divorced eight husbands. On their wedding night, she told him she was still a virgin.
He was just a bit taken aback!

'How come, when you've been married eight times?'

1

'My first husband was in software support.
He was never sure how it was supposed to function, but he said he'd look into it and get back to me.

2

'My second husband was a sales rep.
He kept telling me how great it was going to be.

3

'My third husband was in telemarketing.
He knew he had the order, but he didn't know when he would be able to deliver.

4

'My fourth husband was an engineer.
He understood the process but wanted three years to research and implement a new state-of-the-art method.

5

'My fifth husband was from hardware back-up. He said everything checked out diagnostically but he just couldn't get the system up.

6

'My sixth husband was from administration. He thought he knew how but he wasn't sure whether it was his job or not.

7

'My seventh husband was in marketing. He had a product, but he was never sure how to position it.

8

'My eighth husband was in charge of postage stamps. All he ever did was ... God, I miss him! But now I've married you, I'm really excited!'

'Good,' said the husband, 'but, why?'

'You're a lawyer. This time I know I'm going to get screwed!'

The businessman and his wife were going to decorate their bedroom and were clearing out the drawers in the bedside table. He was a bit embarrassed when she found four golf balls and an envelope containing hundreds of pounds in cash and, of course, she asked him to explain. He couldn't see a way out so he decided to be honest.

'Every time I'm unfaithful to you, I put a golf ball in the drawer.'

His wife was shocked but they had been married a long time and she decided four times in all those years wasn't so bad, but she was still curious.

'So where did all the money come from?' she asked.

'Well, every time I got a dozen, I sold them down the golf club!'

What do blonde typists and the Bermuda triangle have in common?

They've both swallowed a lot of seamen.

What's the difference between a pickpocket and the post-room guy who drilled a hole through the wall in the ladies' room?

A pickpocket snatches watches.

A blonde, a brunette, and a redhead all worked at the same office for a female boss who always went home early on a Friday.

'Hey, girls,' says the brunette, 'let's go home early tomorrow. She'll never know.'

So the next day, they all left right after the boss. The brunette got some extra gardening done, the redhead went to a bar, and the blonde went home to find her husband having sex with the boss! She quietly sneaked out of the house and returned at her normal time.

'We got away with it,' said the brunette. 'We should do it again.'

'No way,' says the blonde. 'I almost got caught.'

The boss was away from the office and went into a business centre.

'I want to send some information to my secretary.'

'Fax?' asked the assistant.

'Not half!' he replied. 'She goes like a bloody train.'

When the body was first made, all the parts wanted to be boss.

The brain said, 'I should be boss because I control everything the body does.'

The feet said, 'We should be boss as we carry the brain about and get it to where it wants to go.'

The hands said, 'We should be the boss because we do all the work and earn all the money.'

And so it went on and on with the heart, the lungs and the eyes.

Finally the asshole spoke up. All the parts laughed at the idea of the asshole being the boss. So the asshole went on strike, blocked itself up and refused to work.

Within a short time the eyes became crossed, the hands clenched, the feet twitched, the heart and lungs began to panic and the brain fevered. Eventually they all decided that the asshole should be the boss, so the motion was passed. All the other parts did all the work while the boss just sat and passed out the shit!

Moral of the story: You don't need brains to be a boss – any asshole will do.

After taking his little girl to work on a take-your-daughter-to-work day, the boss was having dinner with his wife and family.

'I saw you in your office with your secretary today, daddy,' said his daughter. 'Why do you call her a doll?'

Feeling his wife looking at him, the man explained, 'Well, my secretary is a very hard-working girl. She types like you wouldn't believe, she knows the computer system and is very efficient.'

'Oh,' said the little girl, 'I thought it was because she closed her eyes when you lay her down on the desk.'

A secretary goes into her boss's office and asks,
'May I use your dictaphone?'

**'No,' he replied.
'Use your finger like everyone else.'**

A boss was outlining the terms to his new employee.
'I'll give you five pounds an hour starting today and in three months, I'll raise your salary to six pounds an hour.
So when would you like to start?"

'In three months.'

The boss was in the office interviewing a keen young lad for a salesman's job at a major city department store. The boss thought he looked promising, so he decided to give him a trial.

'You can start tomorrow and I'll come and see you when we close.'

It was a long, hard day for the young man, but finally 5 o'clock came round and the boss came to see how he had done.

'How many sales did you make today?' he asked.

'One,' said the young salesman.

'Only one?' blurted out the boss. 'Most of my staff make 20 or 30 sales a day! How much was the sale worth?'

'£100,000,' said the young man.

'How did you manage that?' asked the flabbergasted boss.

'Well,' said the salesman 'this man came in and I sold him a small fish hook, then a medium hook and finally a really large hook. Then I sold him a small fishing line, a medium one and a huge big one. I asked him where he was going fishing and he said down the coast, so I said he would probably need a boat. So I took him down to the boat department and sold him that new schooner with the twin engines. Then he said his Volkswagen probably wouldn't be able to pull it, so I took him to the car department and sold him the new Deluxe Cruiser.'

The boss was seriously impressed! 'You sold all that to a guy who came in for a fish hook?'

'No,' answered the salesman. 'He came in to buy a box of tampons for his wife and I said to him, "Your weekend's shot, you may as well go fishing."'

The blonde came for an interview as a secretary.

'How are you on a word processor?' asked the boss.

'I prefer it on the floor,' she said. 'The keys stick in my back.'

Three office clerks were chatting about their husbands' performance as lovers.

The first woman says, 'My husband works as a marriage counsellor. He always buys me flowers and chocolates before we make love. I like that.'

The second woman says, 'My husband is a motorcycle mechanic. He likes to play rough and slaps me around sometimes. I like that.'

The third woman just shakes her head and says, 'My husband works as an office administrator. He just sits on the edge of the bed and tells me how great it's going to be when I get it.'

Roger came to work Monday and his mate, Ben, asked him how his weekend had gone. He said he had done some gardening and played some golf, so they asked him how well he did.

'Unfortunately, I hit two of my best balls,' he said.

'Why unfortunately?' asked Ben.

'I stepped on a rake.'

An old lady went into a bank carrying a bag of money. She wanted to open a savings account but she would only speak to the manager.

'It's a lot of money!' she kept saying, so eventually they showed her into the manager's office, and he asked her how much she would like to deposit. She emptied the bag on the desk and replied,

'£100,000.'

'I'm surprised you're carrying so much cash around, Madam,' said the manager. 'Where did you get this money?'

The old lady replied, 'I make bets.'

'Bets? What kind of bets?'

'Well, for example, I'll bet you £5,000 that your balls are square.'

'Ha!' laughed the manager, 'that's a stupid bet. You can never win that kind of bet!'

'So would you like to take my bet?' she challenged.

'Certainly,' said the manager.

'Okay,' she replied, 'but since there is a lot of money involved, may I bring my lawyer with me tomorrow at 10 o'clock as a witness?'

'I'll see you then!' replied the confident manager.

That night, however, he began to feel he had been a bit rash and spent a long time in front of a mirror checking his balls.

The next morning, the old lady appeared at the office with her lawyer and introduced the two men.

'£5,000 says your balls are square!' she said to the manager, and asked him to drop his trousers so they could all see. The manager complied. The old lady peered closely at his balls and then asked if she could feel them.

'Well, okay,' said the manager, '£5,000 is a lot of money, so I guess you should be absolutely sure.' Just then, he noticed that the lawyer was quietly banging his head against the wall.

'What the hell's the matter with your lawyer?' he asked.

'I bet him £15,000 that at 10.05 today, I'd have the local bank manager's balls in my hand.'

A man came back from a long business trip to find that his son had an expensive new mountain bike.

'How did you get that, son?'

'By hiking.'

'Hiking?'

'Yeah, every night, mum's boss came over and gave me £30 to take a hike.'

Signs you're burnt out

You're so tired, you answer the phone, 'Hell.'

Your friends call to ask how you've been, and you immediately scream, 'Get off my back, bitch!'

Your waste bin is your 'in' box.

You wake up to discover your bed is on fire, but go back to sleep because you just don't care.

You have so much on your mind, you've forgotten how to pee.

Visions of the weekend help you make it through Monday.

You sleep more at work than at home.

You take your ID badge when you go to the pub.

A woman came home from work wearing a diamond necklace.

'Where did you get that necklace?' asked her husband.

'I won it in a raffle at work,' she replied. 'Go and run me a bath while I start dinner.'

The next day, the woman arrived home wearing a diamond bracelet.

'Where did you get the bracelet?' her husband asked.

'I won it in a raffle at work,' she replied. 'Now go and run my bath while I start dinner.'

The next day, she arrived home wearing an expensive new coat. Beginning to get distinctly suspicious, her husband said,

'I suppose you won that coat in a raffle at work?'

'Yes I did! How did you guess? Go and run my bath while I start supper.'

When she goes up to the bathroom, she notices he's only put an inch of water in the bath.

'Hey!' she yells. 'There's only an inch of water in the bath.'

'I know,' he replies. 'I didn't want you to get your raffle ticket wet.'

Did you hear about the boss who was arrested for flashing?

HIS CASE IS BEING HEARD IN THE SMALL CLAIMS COURT.

What does the boss have in common with an inquisitive dog?

THEY BOTH STICK THEIR NOSES IN THE SECRETARY'S CROTCH.

Office truisms

A bad day fishing is better than a good day at work.

A clean tie attracts the soup of the day.

A good scapegoat is hard to find.

A committee is a group that keeps minutes and loses hours.

A conclusion is the place where you got tired of thinking.

A consultant is an ordinary person a long way from home.

A crisis is when you cannot say 'let's just forget the whole thing'.

A pat on the back is only a few inches from a kick up the arse.

According to the official figures, 43% of all statistics are totally worthless.

Afternoon: the part of the day we spend worrying about how we wasted the morning.

All work and no play will make you a manager.

The boss
returned from
lunch in a
good mood
and called
the whole
staff in to
listen to a couple of
jokes he had picked
up. Everybody, but
one girl laughed
uproariously.

'What's the matter?'
grumbled the boss.
'Haven't you got a
sense of humour?'

'I don't have
to laugh,'
she replied.
'I'm leaving
on Friday.'

A businessman goes to Japan to arrange a deal. After a particularly successful contract, he gets completely bladdered and ends up in bed with a prostitute.

Just as he comes, she cries out something in Japanese,

衆 胞 !

which he decides must be an expression of extreme pleasure.

The next day, he plays a round of golf with his Japanese colleague who manages to score a hole in one. The businessman remembers the phrase and says it to congratulate him.

衆 胞 !

But his colleague is furious.

'What do you mean "wrong hole"?'

A businessman and his wife were having a huge argument over breakfast.

'You aren't so good in bed either,' he shouted at her as he slammed the door and went off to work.

By mid-morning, he thought he ought to ring and apologise so he called home but the phone rang for ages before she answered.

'Why did you take so long to answer?' he asked.

'I was in bed,' she replied.

'What were you doing in bed so late?' he asked.

'Getting a second opinion.'

After the office Christmas party, Pete woke with a thumping headache. He struggled downstairs and slumped into a chair. His wife put a mug of black coffee in front of him.

'Oh God!' he moaned. 'Tell me what happened last night – I can't remember a thing. Was I that bad?'

'Worse,' she replied. 'You made a complete dick of yourself. You infuriated the whole office, upset your secretary and insulted the managing director.'

'He's an arrogant prick. Piss on him!'

'You did – all over his suit,' replied his wife. 'He fired you!'

'Well, fuck him,' Pete said.

'I did,' said his wife. 'You are back at work on Monday.'

Carl was always known for never missing a trick. After their conference, he took two of his colleagues into a strip bar.

Ryan licked a £20 note and stuck it to the lap dancer's butt.

≥ PLIC ≤

Kevin licked a £20 note and stuck it to the other side of her butt.

≥ PLIC ≤

Carl swiped his credit card down her crack and took the £40.

YEP!

The MD was a born exhibitionist and always fancied his chances with the air crew when he travelled abroad. When he was boarding the plane, he opened his coat and exposed himself to the stewardess.

Without batting an eyelid she said,

'I'm sorry, sir. You have to show your ticket here, not your stub.'

A guy came home early from work one afternoon and, since he was feeling horny, he spent a passionate afternoon in bed fucking his wife. They were just about to try out the fifth position in two hours when they heard the sound of a car drawing up outside.

'Quick!' his wife panicked. 'That'll be my husband! Get your clothes on and get out of here!'

The man was so shocked, he began to struggle into his clothes, stuck one leg into his trousers, tripped and fell flat on the floor. That brought him back down to earth in more ways than one.

'What the fuck do you mean by that? I am your husband!'

The office stud thought he was God's gift to women and always chatted up the new staff. This time he struck lucky and Sally agreed to go back to his flat after they'd had a drink at the pub.

He turned down the light, put on some soft music and snuggled up to her on the sofa.'

'You don't talk much,' she said.

'I don't need to,' he boasted, sliding off his trousers to reveal his erect dick. 'This does all the talking for me.'

'Well, that's not saying much either!'

The manager hired a new secretary. One day, while she was taking dictation, she noticed his flies were open. As she left the room, she politely commented,

'Sir, did you know that your barracks door was open.'

Fancying his luck, he thought he'd try to use it to his advantage, so when she was next in the office, he asked her,

'When you saw my barracks door open, did you see a soldier standing to attention?'

'No.' she replied. 'But I did see a little disabled veteran sitting on two duffel bags.'

Resolving to give her husband a pleasant surprise, an executive's wife called into his office on her way home, only to find him with his secretary sitting in his lap.

Without hesitating, he dictated,

'… and in conclusion, gentlemen – shortage or no shortage – I cannot continue to operate this office with just one chair.'

A businessman had the real hots for his secretary. One afternoon, he just couldn't keep it down, and he persuaded her to go to his house for a quick fuck.

'Don't worry,' he told her. 'My wife is out of town on a business trip.'

It wasn't long before their clothes were ripped off and hurled on the floor and things were really getting hot. They were just about to fall into bed when the woman grabbed her handbag and started searching through the contents, getting increasingly desperate.

'We have to stop!' she said. 'I've forgotten to bring a condom!'

'Don't worry,' panted her boss. 'I'll get my wife's diaphragm.'

After a few minutes of searching he came back to the bedroom, beside himself with frustration.

'Stupid bitch!' he shouted. 'She's taken it with her. I knew she didn't trust me!'

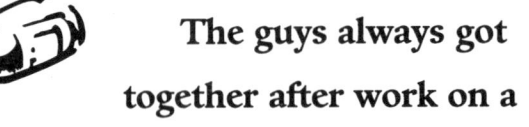

The guys always got together after work on a Friday night for a drink. One Friday, Seb turned up in a foul mood and they asked him what was up.

'My wife told me this week that she's cutting me back to only twice a week ... I can't believe it!'

Bob was reassuring.

'You think you've got problems. She's cut some guys out altogether.'

Office Memorandum

In order to ensure the highest quality work, we intend to keep all employees trained through our Special High Intensity Training (SHIT). We intend to give our employees more SHIT than any other company.

If you feel that you are not receiving your fair share of SHIT on the job, please notify your manager, who is skilled at ensuring you get all the SHIT you can handle.

Employees who do not take their SHIT will be placed in Departmental Employee Evaluation Programmes (DEEP SHIT). Those who fail to take DEEP SHIT seriously will undergo Employee Attitude Training (EAT SHIT). Since our managers took SHIT before promotion, they are already full of SHIT.

If you are full of SHIT, you may be interested in training others. You can sign up to our Basic Understanding Lecture List (BULL SHIT). Those who are full of BULL SHIT will get the SHIT jobs and can apply for promotion from the Director of Intensity Programming (DIP SHIT).

For further information, please contact our Head Of Training, Special High Intensity Training (HOT SHIT).

Boss In General (BIG SHIT)

A married man was having an affair with his secretary. One day, they sneaked out of the office early and spent the afternoon fucking each other senseless in her flat. Finally, they were so exhausted, they fell asleep – and didn't wake up until 8 pm.

'Oh shit!' said Steve as he struggled to find his clothes. 'Quick, take my shoes and rub them in the muddy grass.'

When he finally got home, his wife looked furious.

'Where the hell have you been?'

Steve tried to look apologetic. 'You know I can't lie to you, darling,' he said. 'I am having an affair with my secretary. We spent the whole afternoon making mad, passionate love in her flat. She's such hot stuff, she kept going until I was completely shagged out and I fell asleep.'

His wife looked at his shoes. 'You must think I'm stupid,' she replied. 'Look at the state of your shoes. You've been down that bloody golf course again, haven't you!'

The boss's wife marched into the office brandishing a handful of photographs.

'You filthy tart!' she shouted at the secretary, throwing the photos on the desk. 'You've been screwing around with my husband. I've got a picture of you kissing him in the pub, with his hand on your tits in that fancy new restaurant, and god knows what you are doing in this one in the back of the car! What do you have to say to that?'

'Not bad,' replied the secretary without so much as raising an eyebrow. 'I'll have copies of those for the album.'

Did you hear about the data processor who couldn't get a date for six months?

He's off work with repetitive strain injury.

'It's no good,' moaned the secretary to her boss. 'Your organ is just too small.'

'That's because I'm playing in a bloody cathedral!'

'I'm really hacked off,' the salesman confided to his colleague at the office. 'Everyone seems to take an instant dislike to me. I just can't understand why.'

'Saves time!'

What's the difference between a penis and a bonus?

Your girlfriend will always blow your bonus.

'You'll be expected to perform roughly the same jobs as you did in your last position,' the boss told his new secretary.

'That's fine,' she replied. 'I've got my own pillow to kneel on.'

Two guys were discussing the new secretary at their office.

"I dated her last Tuesday," said Paul. "The sex was brilliant! She's so much better in bed than my wife!"

Two days later, George came into the office.

"Hey, Paul," he said, "I dated that new secretary last night. She's bloody good in the sack - but I still think your wife is better!"

Jim thought he'd done quite well at the interview.

'There is one final part of the selection process,' said the interviewer, 'because you cannot get an erection while you are trying to join this company.' Jim thought it was a bit strange but decided to go along with it. He was asked to undress and tie a bell round his penis, then he went into a room with nine other men, all naked with bells round their penises. Then a naked woman walked through the room.

Nine bells remained quiet, but Jim's was ringing furiously! But the interviewer said he'd give him another chance.

Again, the woman walked through the room, and once again Jim's bell rang.

'I'm sorry,' said the interviewer. 'Pick up your clothes and go. I'm afraid we can't employ you.' So Jim bent down to pick up his clothes and nine bells began to ring!

'It says here you were in the Service,' said the interviewer.

'Yes, I was a Marine,' replied the applicant. 'I was invalided out of the Service and that's why I'm looking for a job.'

'May I ask what happened?'

'A grenade exploded between my legs and I lost both testicles.'

'You're hired!' said the interviewer. 'You can start Monday at 10 am.'

'That seems rather late – when does everyone else start? I don't want any preferential treatment because of my disability.'

'Don't worry about it. Most people get here at 9 but nothing gets done until 10 – we just sit around scratching our balls trying to decide what to do first.'

The drunk was staggering down the road, singing and swearing at the top of his voice. The officer on duty wasn't too impressed.

'Keep the noise down and get on home, mate,' he said, 'or I'll have to arrest you.'

'Ah, but officer, it's my works outing and I'm only trying to enjoy myself.'

'Well, if it's your works outing, where's the rest of them?'

'I work for myself!'